FRENCH COUNTRY
DIARY

FRENCH COUNTRY
DIARY

LINDA DANNENBERG
& GUILLAUME DE LAUBIER

2021

ABRAMS, NEW YORK

*Fabric credits:
All fabric designs, including slipcase, cover fabric, endpapers,
and page borders, are from Les Olivades in Saint-Étienne-du-Grès
and are used with their kind permission.*

*Opposite page:
The charming young Victoire, dressed in a striped frock from
Petite Lucette, the oh-so-chic line of French children's wear,
strolls through a path in the lavender field just below her family's
farmhouse in Sisteron, a town in the Alpes-de-Haute-Provence.*

*Title spread photograph:
The long, stone-bordered pool on Philippe Lizop's handsomely
restored and landscaped Provençal estate near Apt enjoys unimpeded
views southeast toward the Luberon valley.*

*Slipcase photograph:
A pebbled pathway lined with azaleas and sculptural topiaries
leads to the Villa Roxelane, centerpiece of the magnificent Étretat
Gardens set above the seaside village of Étretat.*

Design by Mary Jane Callister

ABRAMS The Art of Books
195 Broadway, New York, NY 10007
abramsbooks.com

Distributed to the trade by Andrews McMeel Publishing, Kansas City, MO

*Printed in China First Printing
ISBN: 978-1-4197-4403-7*

WHEN DRIVING THROUGH the deep countryside of France, it is the unexpected magic revealed at a turn in the road that brings so much joy. There was that early evening in the fall when we were motoring at sunset along an isolated lane leading to a winsome farm village called Sainte-Hélène-Bondeville. The remaining rays of sun gilded the lower leaves of the towering beeches that lined the road, a road that led straight on to the horizon. The sky had turned lavender, and there was not a soul to be seen. This was truly a moment *hors du temps*, timeless. In this year's *French Country Diary,* other country roads lead us to superb gardens we have never visited before, such as the clifftop *Jardins d' Étretat,* the Étretat Gardens in a Norman fishing  village dear to Claude Monet, with sculptures and sculpted topiaries magnificently laid out above the sea. And walking the backcountry of the Alpes-de-Haute-Provence we come upon meticulously groomed and diz- zyingly fragrant lavender fields, at their peak just before harvest. Our itinerary also takes us to the homes of some of France's renowned collectors, such as Jacques and Laurence Darrigade, who have spent decades amassing a vast trove of 19th-century *faience fine* from the Bordelais Manufacture Jules Vieillard, and the de Contades family at their Château de Montgeoffroy in the Loire Valley, with a kitchen gleaming with 250 antique copper pots. And of course, wherever we have been in France, the road always leads us back to Paris. This year not only do we have our traditional "April in Paris" weeks, but winter, summer, and fall weeks in Paris as well, including a Valentine's Day visit to designer Chantal Thomass's seductive pink-and-white *Rive Gauche* apartment, and a sultry summer evening having cocktails on the chic rooftop terrace of the Brach hotel, with a superb view of the twinkling Eiffel Tower across the Seine. How we love this enduring city, and the eternal magic of *La Belle France.*

28 MONDAY
Boxing Day observed
(CAN, UK, AUS, NZ)

29 TUESDAY

30 WEDNESDAY

31 THURSDAY
New Year's Eve
La Saint-Sylvestre (FR)

1 FRIDAY *New Year's Day*

2 SATURDAY

3 SUNDAY

NOTES

An array of French blues, from walls covered in a linen toile to sleek chairs created by renowned interior designer Pierre-Yves Rochon, embellish the dining room of the Rochon family's 19th-century manoir in Brittany.

4 MONDAY *Bank Holiday (SCT, NZ)*

5 TUESDAY

6 WEDNESDAY

7 THURSDAY

8 FRIDAY

9 SATURDAY

10 SUNDAY

NOTES

A majestic 14th-century clock, one of the oldest in France, is the centerpiece of a Renaissance arch above a passageway along the rue du Gros-Horloge in Rouen.

11 MONDAY

15 FRIDAY

12 TUESDAY

16 SATURDAY

13 WEDNESDAY

17 SUNDAY

NOTES

Period elements, such as a pair of Venetian cathedral chairs and a portrait of Cesare Borgia, highlight a 17th-century apartment near Notre-Dame, restored and decorated by designers John Coury and Florent Maillard.

14 THURSDAY

18 MONDAY *Martin Luther King Jr. Day (US)*

19 TUESDAY

20 WEDNESDAY

21 THURSDAY

22 FRIDAY

23 SATURDAY

24 SUNDAY

NOTES

A trinket-and-sweets stand in Paris's Luxembourg Gardens tempts children with pinwheels, whistles, and lollipops from the famous Pierrot Gourmand candy company.

25 MONDAY

29 FRIDAY

26 TUESDAY *Australia Day (AUS)*

30 SATURDAY

27 WEDNESDAY

31 SUNDAY

NOTES

28 THURSDAY

An antique stone fireplace and inviting armchairs covered in Pierre Frey fabric enhance a suite in the Couvent des Herbes, a small restored convent on the grounds of the luxurious resort Les Prés d'Eugénie in Les Landes.

1 MONDAY

5 FRIDAY

2 TUESDAY *Groundhog Day (US, CAN)*

6 SATURDAY *Waitangi Day (NZ)*

3 WEDNESDAY

7 SUNDAY

NOTES

With its 1930s vibe and a menu highlighted by copious seafood platters, the Brasserie Le Central is one of the liveliest restaurants in the resort town of Trouville.

4 THURSDAY

FEBRUARY

8 MONDAY *Waitangi Day observed (NZ)*

9 TUESDAY

10 WEDNESDAY

11 THURSDAY

12 FRIDAY *Lunar New Year (Year of the Ox)*

13 SATURDAY

14 SUNDAY *St. Valentine's Day*

NOTES

The 19th-century shepherdess perched on a living room mantelpiece embodies the romantic charm of designer Chantal Thomass's pink-and-white Paris apartment.

FEBRUARY

15 MONDAY *Presidents' Day (US)*

16 TUESDAY

17 WEDNESDAY *Ash Wednesday*

18 THURSDAY

19 FRIDAY

20 SATURDAY

21 SUNDAY

NOTES

Braquenié fabric from Pierre Frey in a pattern called Aix-en-Provence and Louis XVI furniture create a sumptuous bedroom at the 18th-century Château de Montgeoffroy, an aristocratic Loire Valley residence of the de Contades family.

22 MONDAY

23 TUESDAY

24 WEDNESDAY

25 THURSDAY *Purim (begins at sundown)*

26 FRIDAY

27 SATURDAY

28 SUNDAY

NOTES

The turreted and heavily fortified Renaissance Château de Bannes, built in the late 1400s, dominates a hillside in the Dordogne town of Beaumontois-en-Périgord.

1 MONDAY

2 TUESDAY

3 WEDNESDAY

4 THURSDAY

5 FRIDAY

6 SATURDAY

7 SUNDAY

NOTES

A French Gaveau baby grand piano in mahogany and lemon-wood takes center stage in the music room of designer Pierre Yovanovitch's Provençal estate; on the right is a 1930s leather sofa by Danish designer Frits Henningsen.

8 MONDAY
Commonwealth Day (CAN, UK, AUS, NZ)

9 TUESDAY

10 WEDNESDAY

11 THURSDAY

12 FRIDAY

13 SATURDAY

14 SUNDAY
Daylight Saving Time begins (US, CAN)
Mothering Sunday (UK, IRL)

NOTES

A cozy guest cottage at the rustic hotel D'Une Île in Rémalard, a village in Normandy's Perche region, was once part of a sprawling 17th-century family farm.

MARCH

15 MONDAY

16 TUESDAY

17 WEDNESDAY *St. Patrick's Day*

18 THURSDAY

19 FRIDAY

20 SATURDAY *Vernal Equinox*

21 SUNDAY

NOTES

A lavishly decorated 17th-century Portuguese armoire and vine-enlaced chairs, created for a noble Italian family, complement each other in the dining room of esteemed antiques dealer Pierre Passebon's Paris apartment.

22 MONDAY

23 TUESDAY

24 WEDNESDAY

25 THURSDAY

26 FRIDAY

27 SATURDAY
Passover (begins at sundown)

28 SUNDAY
Palm Sunday
Summer Time begins (UK, IRL)

NOTES

The Gothic spires of the Bayeux Cathedral, consecrated in 1077 in the presence of William the Conqueror, soar to the sky in the heart of Normandy's historic Bayeux.

29 MONDAY

30 TUESDAY

31 WEDNESDAY

1 THURSDAY *April Fools' Day*

2 FRIDAY *Good Friday*

3 SATURDAY

4 SUNDAY *Easter Sunday*

NOTES

Elements of neoclassical Louis XVI style, among them the urn-and-garland bas-relief inset above the door and the hand-forged pendant lantern, embellish the oval dining room of the Loire Valley's Château de Montgeoffroy.

APRIL

5 MONDAY *Easter Monday*

6 TUESDAY

7 WEDNESDAY

8 THURSDAY

9 FRIDAY

10 SATURDAY

11 SUNDAY

NOTES

The iconic Paris Metro station, Palais Royal-Musée du Louvre on the rue de Rivoli, was designed in 1900 by influential Art Nouveau architect Hector Guimard.

12 MONDAY *Ramadan begins*

13 TUESDAY

14 WEDNESDAY

15 THURSDAY

16 FRIDAY

17 SATURDAY

18 SUNDAY

NOTES

The warm and inviting contemporary décor by Philippe Starck, and a Mediterranean-inspired menu from chef Adam Bentalha, draw a chic Parisian crowd to the lively restaurant Brach in the 16th arrondissement.

APRIL

19 MONDAY

20 TUESDAY

21 WEDNESDAY

22 THURSDAY *Earth Day*

23 FRIDAY

24 SATURDAY

25 SUNDAY *Anzac Day (AUS, NZ)*

NOTES

These classic Luxembourg Gardens armchairs, designed in 1923 and reinterpreted today by the French firm Fermob, are placed under the trees in this beautiful Paris park.

26 MONDAY *Anzac Day observed (AUS, NZ)*

27 TUESDAY

28 WEDNESDAY

29 THURSDAY

30 FRIDAY

1 SATURDAY

2 SUNDAY

NOTES

Breakfast is served in an elegant suite at the Cour des Vosges, a luxurious Paris hotel set in a 17th-century mansion overlooking the historic Place des Vosges, a noble enclave commissioned in the early 1600s by King Henri IV.

MAY

3 MONDAY *Early May Bank Holiday (UK, IRL)*

4 TUESDAY

5 WEDNESDAY

6 THURSDAY

7 FRIDAY

8 SATURDAY

9 SUNDAY *Mother's Day (US, CAN, AUS, NZ)*

NOTES

A pebbled pathway lined with azaleas and sculptural topiaries leads to the Villa Roxelane, centerpiece of the magnificent Jardins d'Étretat set above the seaside village of Étretat.

10 MONDAY

11 TUESDAY

12 WEDNESDAY *Eid al-Fitr begins*

13 THURSDAY

14 FRIDAY

15 SATURDAY

16 SUNDAY

NOTES

A rare collection of 19th-century figurative plates, vases, and objects, many from the Manufacture Jules Vieillard, covers the walls in the home of renowned Bordeaux faience collectors Jacques and Laurence Darrigade.

17 MONDAY

18 TUESDAY

19 WEDNESDAY

20 THURSDAY

21 FRIDAY

22 SATURDAY

23 SUNDAY

NOTES

Les Cigognes ("The Storks"), a thatched-roof farmhouse and bed-and-breakfast in the countryside of the Marais-Vernier near Honfleur, is a dream of springtime in Normandy, with apple trees in bloom and nesting storks.

24 MONDAY *Victoria Day (CAN)*

25 TUESDAY

26 WEDNESDAY

27 THURSDAY

28 FRIDAY

29 SATURDAY

30 SUNDAY

NOTES

In contrast with the predominately pink-and-white palette that graces most of her Paris apartment, designer Chantal Thomass chooses a striking black for her kitchen along with pink accents to highlight cabinets and chairs.

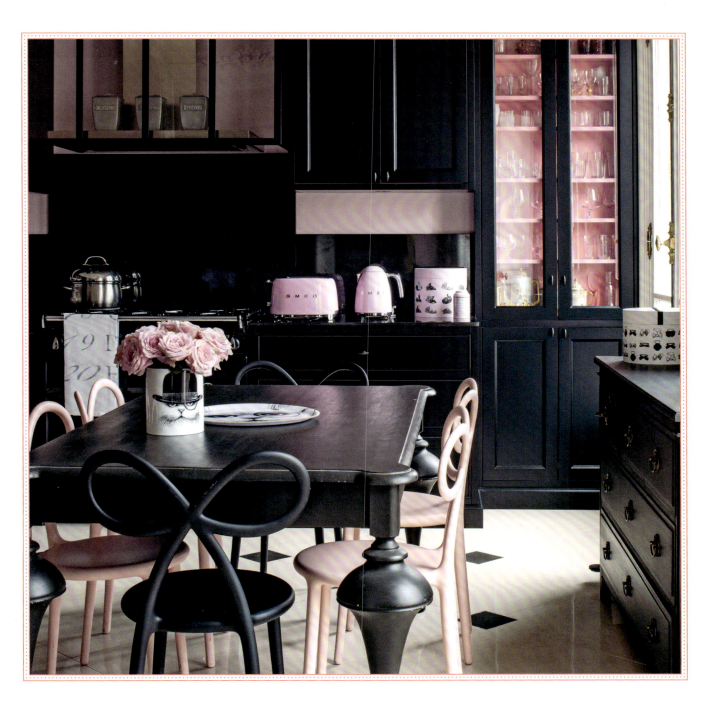

31 MONDAY
Memorial Day (US)
Spring Bank Holiday (UK)

1 TUESDAY

2 WEDNESDAY

3 THURSDAY

4 FRIDAY

5 SATURDAY

6 SUNDAY

NOTES

A well-used market basket filled with fresh lilacs from the garden is always part of the weekend scene at designer Sarah Lavoine's Gascogne farmhouse in France's southwest.

JUNE

7 MONDAY
Bank Holiday (IRL)
Queen's Birthday (NZ)

8 TUESDAY

9 WEDNESDAY

10 THURSDAY

11 FRIDAY

12 SATURDAY

13 SUNDAY

NOTES

A serpentine road leads up to the Domaine Saint-Clair Le Donjon, a Belle Epoque manor house, now reborn as a hotel with lush gardens and atmospheric rooms, overlooking the chalk cliffs of the Alabaster Coast in Étretat.

14 MONDAY *Flag Day (US)*

15 TUESDAY

16 WEDNESDAY

17 THURSDAY

18 FRIDAY

19 SATURDAY

20 SUNDAY
Summer Solstice
Father's Day (US, CAN, UK, IRL)

NOTES

A treasured family album of early 20th-century photographs inspires a nostalgic moment at the home of an art historian in Burgundy.

21 MONDAY

22 TUESDAY

23 WEDNESDAY

24 THURSDAY

25 FRIDAY

26 SATURDAY

27 SUNDAY

NOTES

The cliff-top Notre-Dame-de-la-Garde, a granite-and-slate chapel on the Normandy coast west of Le Havre, was built in the mid-1800s by shipwrights to honor the region's sailors.

28 MONDAY

29 TUESDAY

30 WEDNESDAY

1 THURSDAY *Canada Day (CAN)*

2 FRIDAY

3 SATURDAY

4 SUNDAY *Independence Day (US)*

NOTES

Navigated by little children with long sticks, handmade vintage toy sailboats that ply the waters of the Luxembourg Gardens' octagonal Grand Bassin have been a source of happy childhood memories since the late 1800s.

5 MONDAY *Independence Day observed (US)*

6 TUESDAY

7 WEDNESDAY

8 THURSDAY

9 FRIDAY

10 SATURDAY

11 SUNDAY

NOTES

A limestone gardener's cottage is the focal point of a vast field of lavender on a farm near Sisteron in the Alpes-de-Haute-Provence, a rich agricultural region.

12 MONDAY *Orangemen's Day (N. IRL)*

16 FRIDAY

13 TUESDAY

17 SATURDAY

14 WEDNESDAY
Bastille Day/La Fête Nationale (FR)

18 SUNDAY

NOTES

The vivid, whimsical art of French designer Jean-Charles de Castelbajac adorns the walls and chairs in the sea-themed dining room of the restaurant Le Donjon in Étretat.

15 THURSDAY

19 MONDAY *Eid al-Adha begins*

20 TUESDAY

21 WEDNESDAY

22 THURSDAY

23 FRIDAY

24 SATURDAY

25 SUNDAY

NOTES

Sunset burnishes the granite façade of the 17th-century Château de Vauville, a property famed for its botanical gardens on the western coast of the Cotentin Peninsula.

26 MONDAY

30 FRIDAY

27 TUESDAY

31 SATURDAY

28 WEDNESDAY

1 SUNDAY

NOTES

29 THURSDAY

An undulating bamboo canopy provides translucent shade for a table laid with festive striped linens at decorator Sarah Lavoine's southwestern farmhouse in the Gers.

2 MONDAY
Civic Holiday (CAN)
Bank Holiday (SCT, IRL)

3 TUESDAY

4 WEDNESDAY

5 THURSDAY

6 FRIDAY

7 SATURDAY

8 SUNDAY

NOTES

A green-capped lighthouse guards the granite-walled harbor of Le Palais, the largest town on Brittany's ruggedly beautiful island of Belle-Île.

9 MONDAY

10 TUESDAY

11 WEDNESDAY

12 THURSDAY

13 FRIDAY

14 SATURDAY

15 SUNDAY

NOTES

The cozy rooftop terrace that crowns the contemporary-chic Brach hotel in the 16th arrondissement is the perfect spot to enjoy cocktails, conversation, and a remarkable view of the Eiffel Tower.

16 MONDAY

17 TUESDAY

18 WEDNESDAY

19 THURSDAY

20 FRIDAY

21 SATURDAY

22 SUNDAY

NOTES

A grouping of blue-and-white French 19th-century faience fine features prominently in the tiled kitchen of Bordeaux collectors Jacques and Laurence Darrigade.

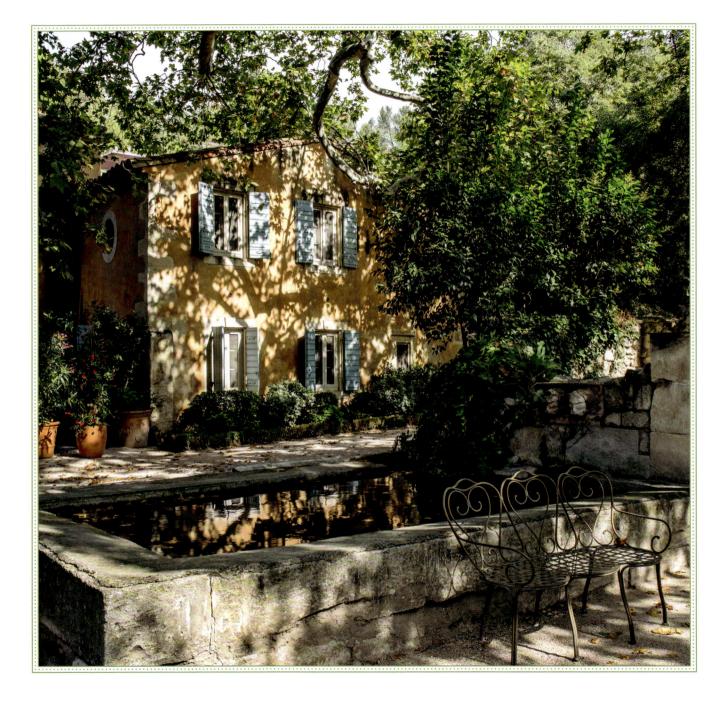

23 MONDAY

24 TUESDAY

25 WEDNESDAY

26 THURSDAY

27 FRIDAY

28 SATURDAY

29 SUNDAY

NOTES

Le Manoir, an auberge on the property of the famed L'Oustau de Baumanière in Les Baux-de-Provence, retains the esprit of its roots as a noble 18th-century country house.

30 MONDAY
Summer Bank Holiday (UK, except SCT)

31 TUESDAY

1 WEDNESDAY

2 THURSDAY

3 FRIDAY

4 SATURDAY

5 SUNDAY *Father's Day (AUS, NZ)*

NOTES

A custom-designed sofa, set beneath a painted screen by French artist and engraver Jean-Émile Laboureur, faces a copper-and-bronze table by sculptor Claude Lalanne in the luminous Paris apartment of antiques dealer Pierre Passebon.

6 MONDAY
Rosh Hashanah (begins at sundown)
Labor Day (US, CAN)

7 TUESDAY

8 WEDNESDAY

9 THURSDAY

10 FRIDAY

11 SATURDAY

12 SUNDAY

NOTES

A ceremonial double staircase leads to the entrance of the 18th-century Château de Bois-Héroult, an edifice of brick, stone, and slate surrounded by 54 acres of French gardens and reflecting pools, in Normandy's Pays de Caux.

13 MONDAY

14 TUESDAY

15 WEDNESDAY
Yom Kippur (begins at sundown)

16 THURSDAY

17 FRIDAY

18 SATURDAY

19 SUNDAY

NOTES

In the stone-walled kitchen of the Manoncourt family's Château Figéac, antique copperware, mullioned windows, and a vintage potager (or hob stove), speak to the history of this St. Émilion Grand-Cru Classé estate, founded in 1780.

20 MONDAY

21 TUESDAY

22 WEDNESDAY *Autumnal Equinox*

23 THURSDAY

24 FRIDAY

25 SATURDAY

26 SUNDAY

NOTES

The old Port of Honfleur, with its tall, slate-roofed, half-timbered houses, has long charmed artists from Monet to Braque and was the 17th-century setting for Samuel de Champlain's historic departures to explore the New World.

27 MONDAY

28 TUESDAY

29 WEDNESDAY

30 THURSDAY

1 FRIDAY

2 SATURDAY

3 SUNDAY

NOTES

A Louis XVI sofa upholstered in flocked orange velour provides a dazzling contrast to the custom, blue-paneled walls and "Pia" rug from Casa Lopez in executive Pierre Sauvage's 18th-century Left Bank apartment.

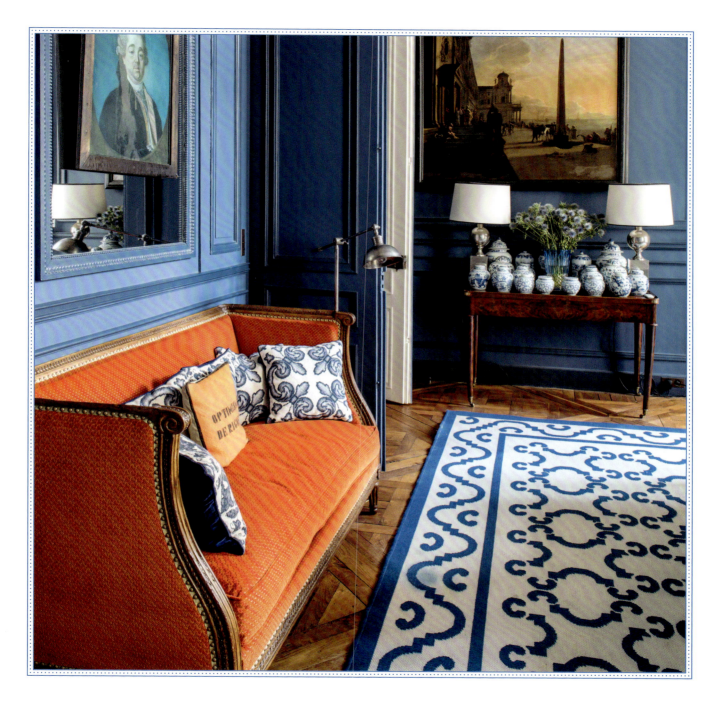

4 MONDAY

5 TUESDAY

6 WEDNESDAY

7 THURSDAY

8 FRIDAY

9 SATURDAY

10 SUNDAY

NOTES

A dreamlike ribbon of rural road lined with towering beech trees winds its way to the horizon in the small farming commune of Sainte-Hélène-Bondeville, a short drive north-east of Le Havre.

11 MONDAY
Columbus Day (US)
Thanksgiving Day (CAN)

12 TUESDAY

13 WEDNESDAY

14 THURSDAY

15 FRIDAY

16 SATURDAY

17 SUNDAY

NOTES

Bouquets of vintage spoons and ladles stand tall in ceramic pots and mugs in the Paris kitchen of French designer and collector Daniel Rozensztroch.

18 MONDAY

19 TUESDAY

20 WEDNESDAY

21 THURSDAY

22 FRIDAY

23 SATURDAY

24 SUNDAY

NOTES

The vestiges of a medieval pavilion with two towers and an enclosed balcony mark the entrance to the Manoir de la Pommeraye, a private Norman country house near Honfleur.

25 MONDAY
Bank Holiday (IRL)
Labour Day (NZ)

26 TUESDAY

27 WEDNESDAY

28 THURSDAY

29 FRIDAY

30 SATURDAY

31 SUNDAY
Halloween
Summer Time ends (UK, IRL)

NOTES

A passion for parrots is evident in paintings, on plates, and in porcelain figurines throughout the Dieppe home of artist and collector Mathias Toulemonde.

NOVEMBER

1 MONDAY
All Saints' Day/La Toussaint (FR)

2 TUESDAY *Election Day (US)*

3 WEDNESDAY

4 THURSDAY *Diwali*

5 FRIDAY

6 SATURDAY

7 SUNDAY
Daylight Saving Time ends (US, CAN)

NOTES

The tightly clustered antique houses of Domfront, a historic town a short drive east of the Mont Saint-Michel, were once enclosed within a turreted medieval wall.

8 MONDAY

9 TUESDAY

10 WEDNESDAY

THURSDAY
Veterans Day (US)
Remembrance Day (CAN)
11 *Armistice Day* (FR)

12 FRIDAY

13 SATURDAY

14 SUNDAY *Remembrance Sunday* (UK)

NOTES

Egyptian motifs, favored by Napoleon, characterize much of Empire style, as exemplified by these fauteuils crafted for Napoleon's uncle Cardinal Fesch and today in the collection of Empire expert Pierre-Jean Chalençon.

NOVEMBER

15 MONDAY

16 TUESDAY

17 WEDNESDAY

18 THURSDAY

19 FRIDAY

20 SATURDAY

21 SUNDAY

NOTES

These antique porcelain demi-figurines, sometimes described as half-dolls, from the collection of noted Paris lawyer Jacqueline Socquet-Clerc Lafont, were usually fitted with lavish hoop skirts to serve as tea cozies or covers for a variety of boxes.

22 MONDAY

23 TUESDAY

24 WEDNESDAY

25 THURSDAY *Thanksgiving Day (US)*

26 FRIDAY

27 SATURDAY

28 SUNDAY
Hanukkah (begins at sundown)

NOTES

More than 250 pieces of gleaming 18th-century copperware line the walls of the vast kitchen at the historic Château de Montgeoffroy in the Loire Valley village of Mazé-Milon.

29 MONDAY

30 TUESDAY *St. Andrew's Day (SCT)*

1 WEDNESDAY

2 THURSDAY

3 FRIDAY

4 SATURDAY

5 SUNDAY

NOTES

A rare Empire-style chair by ébeniste Georges Jacob is nestled by a window in art expert Rémy Le Fur's Right Bank Paris apartment overlooking the Tuileries Garden and the Louvre.

6 MONDAY

7 TUESDAY

8 WEDNESDAY

9 THURSDAY

10 FRIDAY

11 SATURDAY

12 SUNDAY

NOTES

Every day there are at least 30 varieties of chocolate bonbons—chocolate-dipped orange slices, pastilles, nougats—at the shop of Charles Bataille, chocolatier extraordinaire, in the Perche village of Bellême.

13 MONDAY

14 TUESDAY

15 WEDNESDAY

16 THURSDAY

17 FRIDAY

18 SATURDAY

19 SUNDAY

NOTES

Les Fermes de Marie, a luxurious, chalet-style Alpine resort in the mountains of Megève, takes on a festive air with sparkling Christmas lights reflected in the new-fallen snow.

20 MONDAY

21 TUESDAY *Winter Solstice*

22 WEDNESDAY

23 THURSDAY

24 FRIDAY *Christmas Day observed (US)*

25 SATURDAY *Christmas Day*

26 SUNDAY
Kwanzaa begins (US)
Boxing Day (CAN, UK, AUS, NZ)
St. Stephen's Day (FR, IRL, WLS)

NOTES

Designer Alexandre Zouari credits the inspiration of his muse and longtime friend Madeleine Castaing, the iconic French designer, for the rose-and-jade palette and sumptuous mix of patterned fabrics in his Normandy country home.

27 MONDAY
Christmas Day observed (CAN, UK, AUS, NZ)

28 TUESDAY
Boxing Day observed (CAN, UK, AUS, NZ)

29 WEDNESDAY

30 THURSDAY

31 FRIDAY
New Year's Eve
La Saint-Sylvestre (FR)

1 SATURDAY *New Year's Day*

2 SUNDAY

NOTES

The 18th-century furnishings in the Château de Montgeof-froy, surviving revolutions and world wars, are original to the 1775 property, including these Louis XV fauteuils and the beveled blue paneling.

2021

JANUARY

S	M	T	W	T	F	S
					1	2
3	4	5	6	7	8	9
10	11	12	13	14	15	16
17	18	19	20	21	22	23
24/31	25	26	27	28	29	30

FEBRUARY

S	M	T	W	T	F	S
	1	2	3	4	5	6
7	8	9	10	11	12	13
14	15	16	17	18	19	20
21	22	23	24	25	26	27
28						

MARCH

S	M	T	W	T	F	S
	1	2	3	4	5	6
7	8	9	10	11	12	13
14	15	16	17	18	19	20
21	22	23	24	25	26	27
28	29	30	31			

APRIL

S	M	T	W	T	F	S
				1	2	3
4	5	6	7	8	9	10
11	12	13	14	15	16	17
18	19	20	21	22	23	24
25	26	27	28	29	30	

Window décor at Étretat's Domaine Saint-Clair Le Donjon Hotel

MAY

S	M	T	W	T	F	S
						1
2	3	4	5	6	7	8
9	10	11	12	13	14	15
16	17	18	19	20	21	22
23/30	24/31	25	26	27	28	29

JUNE

S	M	T	W	T	F	S
		1	2	3	4	5
6	7	8	9	10	11	12
13	14	15	16	17	18	19
20	21	22	23	24	25	26
27	28	29	30			

JULY

S	M	T	W	T	F	S
				1	2	3
4	5	6	7	8	9	10
11	12	13	14	15	16	17
18	19	20	21	22	23	24
25	26	27	28	29	30	31

AUGUST

S	M	T	W	T	F	S
1	2	3	4	5	6	7
8	9	10	11	12	13	14
15	16	17	18	19	20	21
22	23	24	25	26	27	28
29	30	31				

SEPTEMBER

S	M	T	W	T	F	S
			1	2	3	4
5	6	7	8	9	10	11
12	13	14	15	16	17	18
19	20	21	22	23	24	25
26	27	28	29	30		

OCTOBER

S	M	T	W	T	F	S
					1	2
3	4	5	6	7	8	9
10	11	12	13	14	15	16
17	18	19	20	21	22	23
24/31	25	26	27	28	29	30

NOVEMBER

S	M	T	W	T	F	S
	1	2	3	4	5	6
7	8	9	10	11	12	13
14	15	16	17	18	19	20
21	22	23	24	25	26	27
28	29	30				

DECEMBER

S	M	T	W	T	F	S
			1	2	3	4
5	6	7	8	9	10	11
12	13	14	15	16	17	18
19	20	21	22	23	24	25
26	27	28	29	30	31	

2022

JANUARY

S	M	T	W	T	F	S
						1
2	3	4	5	6	7	8
9	10	11	12	13	14	15
16	17	18	19	20	21	22
23/30	24/31	25	26	27	28	29

MARCH

S	M	T	W	T	F	S
		1	2	3	4	5
6	7	8	9	10	11	12
13	14	15	16	17	18	19
20	21	22	23	24	25	26
27	28	29	30	31		

A Saint-Louis vase and Chinese pots chez Pierre Sauvage in Paris

FEBRUARY

S	M	T	W	T	F	S
		1	2	3	4	5
6	7	8	9	10	11	12
13	14	15	16	17	18	19
20	21	22	23	24	25	26
27	28					

APRIL

S	M	T	W	T	F	S
					1	2
3	4	5	6	7	8	9
10	11	12	13	14	15	16
17	18	19	20	21	22	23
24	25	26	27	28	29	30

MAY

S	M	T	W	T	F	S
1	2	3	4	5	6	7
8	9	10	11	12	13	14
15	16	17	18	19	20	21
22	23	24	25	26	27	28
29	30	31				

JUNE

S	M	T	W	T	F	S
			1	2	3	4
5	6	7	8	9	10	11
12	13	14	15	16	17	18
19	20	21	22	23	24	25
26	27	28	29	30		

JULY

S	M	T	W	T	F	S
					1	2
3	4	5	6	7	8	9
10	11	12	13	14	15	16
17	18	19	20	21	22	23
24/31	25	26	27	28	29	30

AUGUST

S	M	T	W	T	F	S
	1	2	3	4	5	6
7	8	9	10	11	12	13
14	15	16	17	18	19	20
21	22	23	24	25	26	27
28	29	30	31			

SEPTEMBER

S	M	T	W	T	F	S
				1	2	3
4	5	6	7	8	9	10
11	12	13	14	15	16	17
18	19	20	21	22	23	24
25	26	27	28	29	30	

OCTOBER

S	M	T	W	T	F	S
						1
2	3	4	5	6	7	8
9	10	11	12	13	14	15
16	17	18	19	20	21	22
23/30	24/31	25	26	27	28	29

NOVEMBER

S	M	T	W	T	F	S
		1	2	3	4	5
6	7	8	9	10	11	12
13	14	15	16	17	18	19
20	21	22	23	24	25	26
27	28	29	30			

DECEMBER

S	M	T	W	T	F	S
				1	2	3
4	5	6	7	8	9	10
11	12	13	14	15	16	17
18	19	20	21	22	23	24
25	26	27	28	29	30	31

A · B

NAME ....
Address ....

....
Phone   *Mobile* ....
Email ....

NAME ....
Address ....

....
Phone   *Mobile* ....
Email ....

NAME ....
Address ....

....
Phone   *Mobile* ....
Email ....

NAME ....
Address ....

....
Phone   *Mobile* ....
Email ....

NAME ....
Address ....

....
Phone   *Mobile* ....
Email ....

NAME ....
Address ....

....
Phone   *Mobile* ....
Email ....

NAME ....
Address ....

....
Phone   *Mobile* ....
Email ....

NAME ....
Address ....

....
Phone   *Mobile* ....
Email ....

NAME ....
Address ....

....
Phone   *Mobile* ....
Email ....

NAME ....
Address ....

....
Phone   *Mobile* ....
Email ....

C · D

NAME	**NAME**
Address	*Address*
Phone　　　　*Mobile*	*Phone*　　　　*Mobile*
Email	*Email*
NAME	**NAME**
Address	*Address*
Phone　　　　*Mobile*	*Phone*　　　　*Mobile*
Email	*Email*
NAME	**NAME**
Address	*Address*
Phone　　　　*Mobile*	*Phone*　　　　*Mobile*
Email	*Email*
NAME	**NAME**
Address	*Address*
Phone　　　　*Mobile*	*Phone*　　　　*Mobile*
Email	*Email*
NAME	**NAME**
Address	*Address*
Phone　　　　*Mobile*	*Phone*　　　　*Mobile*
Email	*Email*

E·F

NAME

Address

Phone   Mobile

Email

NAME

Address

Phone   Mobile

Email

NAME

Address

Phone   Mobile

Email

NAME

Address

Phone   Mobile

Email

NAME

Address

Phone   Mobile

Email

NAME

Address

Phone   Mobile

Email

NAME

Address

Phone   Mobile

Email

NAME

Address

Phone   Mobile

Email

NAME

Address

Phone   Mobile

Email

NAME

Address

Phone   Mobile

Email

G·H

NAME	**NAME**
Address	*Address*
Phone　　　　*Mobile*	*Phone*　　　　*Mobile*
Email	*Email*
NAME	**NAME**
Address	*Address*
Phone　　　　*Mobile*	*Phone*　　　　*Mobile*
Email	*Email*
NAME	**NAME**
Address	*Address*
Phone　　　　*Mobile*	*Phone*　　　　*Mobile*
Email	*Email*
NAME	**NAME**
Address	*Address*
Phone　　　　*Mobile*	*Phone*　　　　*Mobile*
Email	*Email*
NAME	**NAME**
Address	*Address*
Phone　　　　*Mobile*	*Phone*　　　　*Mobile*
Email	*Email*

I · J

NAME
....

Address
....

....

Phone   *Mobile*
....

Email
....

NAME
....

Address
....

....

Phone   *Mobile*
....

Email
....

NAME
....

Address
....

....

Phone   *Mobile*
....

Email
....

NAME
....

Address
....

....

Phone   *Mobile*
....

Email
....

NAME
....

Address
....

....

Phone   *Mobile*
....

Email
....

NAME
....

Address
....

....

Phone   *Mobile*
....

Email
....

NAME
....

Address
....

....

Phone   *Mobile*
....

Email
....

NAME
....

Address
....

....

Phone   *Mobile*
....

Email
....

NAME
....

Address
....

....

Phone   *Mobile*
....

Email
....

NAME
....

Address
....

....

Phone   *Mobile*
....

Email
....

NAME
....

Address
....

....

Phone .... *Mobile* ....

Email ....

NAME
....

Address
....

....

Phone .... *Mobile* ....

Email ....

NAME
....

Address
....

....

Phone .... *Mobile* ....

Email ....

NAME
....

Address
....

....

Phone .... *Mobile* ....

Email ....

NAME
....

Address
....

....

Phone .... *Mobile* ....

Email ....

NAME
....

Address
....

....

Phone .... *Mobile* ....

Email ....

NAME
....

Address
....

....

Phone .... *Mobile* ....

Email ....

NAME
....

Address
....

....

Phone .... *Mobile* ....

Email ....

NAME
....

Address
....

....

Phone .... *Mobile* ....

Email ....

NAME
....

Address
....

....

Phone .... *Mobile* ....

Email ....

M · N

NAME
....
Address
....
....
Phone   *Mobile*
....
Email
....

NAME
....
Address
....
....
Phone   *Mobile*
....
Email
....

NAME
....
Address
....
....
Phone   *Mobile*
....
Email
....

NAME
....
Address
....
....
Phone   *Mobile*
....
Email
....

NAME
....
Address
....
....
Phone   *Mobile*
....
Email
....

NAME
....
Address
....
....
Phone   *Mobile*
....
Email
....

NAME
....
Address
....
....
Phone   *Mobile*
....
Email
....

NAME
....
Address
....
....
Phone   *Mobile*
....
Email
....

NAME
....
Address
....
....
Phone   *Mobile*
....
Email
....

NAME
....
Address
....
....
Phone   *Mobile*
....
Email
....

O · P

NAME
....
Address
....

....
Phone   *Mobile*
Email
....

NAME
....
Address
....

....
Phone   *Mobile*
Email
....

NAME
....
Address
....

....
Phone   *Mobile*
Email
....

NAME
....
Address
....

....
Phone   *Mobile*
Email
....

NAME
....
Address
....

....
Phone   *Mobile*
Email
....

NAME
....
Address
....

....
Phone   *Mobile*
Email
....

NAME
....
Address
....

....
Phone   *Mobile*
Email
....

NAME
....
Address
....

....
Phone   *Mobile*
Email
....

NAME
....
Address
....

....
Phone   *Mobile*
Email
....

NAME
....
Address
....

....
Phone   *Mobile*
Email
....

Q · R

NAME

Address

Phone   *Mobile*

Email

NAME

Address

Phone   *Mobile*

Email

NAME

Address

Phone   *Mobile*

Email

NAME

Address

Phone   *Mobile*

Email

NAME

Address

Phone   *Mobile*

Email

NAME

Address

Phone   *Mobile*

Email

NAME

Address

Phone   *Mobile*

Email

NAME

Address

Phone   *Mobile*

Email

NAME

Address

Phone   *Mobile*

Email

NAME

Address

Phone   *Mobile*

Email

S·T

NAME

Address

Phone   Mobile

Email

NAME

Address

Phone   Mobile

Email

NAME

Address

Phone   Mobile

Email

NAME

Address

Phone   Mobile

Email

NAME

Address

Phone   Mobile

Email

NAME

Address

Phone   Mobile

Email

NAME

Address

Phone   Mobile

Email

NAME

Address

Phone   Mobile

Email

NAME

Address

Phone   Mobile

Email

NAME

Address

Phone   Mobile

Email

U·V·W

NAME

Address

Phone   Mobile

Email

NAME

Address

Phone   Mobile

Email

NAME

Address

Phone   Mobile

Email

NAME

Address

Phone   Mobile

Email

NAME

Address

Phone   Mobile

Email

NAME

Address

Phone   Mobile

Email

NAME

Address

Phone   Mobile

Email

NAME

Address

Phone   Mobile

Email

NAME

Address

Phone   Mobile

Email

NAME

Address

Phone   Mobile

Email

X·Y·Z

NAME

Address

Phone   Mobile

Email

NAME

Address

Phone   Mobile

Email

NAME

Address

Phone   Mobile

Email

NAME

Address

Phone   Mobile

Email

NAME

Address

Phone   Mobile

Email

NAME

Address

Phone   Mobile

Email

NAME

Address

Phone   Mobile

Email

NAME

Address

Phone   Mobile

Email

NAME

Address

Phone   Mobile

Email

NAME

Address

Phone   Mobile

Email

SPECIAL EVENTS

SOURCES

All telephone numbers are listed for dialing within France. When calling internationally from outside of France, use your country's international access code (011 in the United States for example), dial "33" for France, then drop the first "0" of the listed number.

FABRICS: All of the fabric designs featured in these pages are from Les Olivades, the French textile company in Saint-Étienne-du-Grès. *Les Olivades*, Chemin des Indienneurs, 13103 Saint-Étienne-du-Grès; Tel: 04-90-49-19-19; www.lesolivades.com

DECEMBER 28–JANUARY 3: Pierre-Yves Rochon is one of France's most eminent interior designers, known particularly for his luxurious hotel projects and restaurant interiors. *Pierre-Yves Rochon*, 9 avenue Matignon, 75008 Paris; Tel: 01-44-95-84-84; pyr-design.com

JANUARY 11–17: The design firm of John Coury and Florent Maillard, CM Studio Paris, specializes in handsome, period-perfect restorations and décor. *CM Studio Paris*, 58 rue Quincampoix, 75004 Paris; contact@cmstudioparis.com; cmstudioparis.com

JANUARY 25–31: Michel Guérard's Les Prés d'Eugénie offers three-star cuisine, a posh spa, and some of the most romantic rooms in France. *Les Prés d'Eugénie, Michel Guérard*, 234 rue René Vielle, 40320 Eugénie-les-Bains; Tel: 05-58-05-06-07; lespresdeugenie.com

FEBRUARY 1–7: The Brasserie Le Central offers a large menu of seafood selections as well as classic bistro fare.

Brasserie Le Central, 158 boulevard Fernand Moureaux, 14360 Trouville; Tel: 02-31-88-13-68; groupe-hvc.com

FEBRUARY 8–14: Chantal Thomass is a designer known for her romantic spirit and her seductive lines of lingerie. *Chantal Thomass,* 211 rue Saint-Honoré, 75001 Paris; Tel: 01-42-60-40-56; chantalthomass.com

FEBRUARY 15–21: The Château de Montgeoffroy, set in the Anjou region east of Angers, is a superb time capsule of 18th-century aristocratic style. The château hosts guided visits and special events. *Château de Montgeoffroy*, route de Seiches, 49630 Mazé-Milon; Tel: 06-42-33-68-07; chateaudemontgeoffroy.com

MARCH 1–7: Pierre Yovanovitch is a celebrated interior designer known for his warm, minimalist interiors, the richness of his basic materials—rare woods, stone, leather—and the sculptural forms of his furniture. *Pierre Yovanovitch Architecture d'Intérieur*, 6 rue Beauregard, 75002 Paris; Tel: 01-42-66-33-98; pierreyovanovitch.com

MARCH 8–14: While the setting is rustic at D'Une Île, a small hotel on a historic farm in Le Perche, chef Bertrand Grébaut's cuisine is world-class. Meals at the inn's small wooden tables are prepared with finesse using local ingredients. *D'Une Île*, Domaine de L'Aulnay, 61110 Rémalard; Tel: 02-33-83-01-47; duneile.com

MARCH 15–21: Pierre Passebon, an esteemed Paris *antiquaire*, specializes in rare 20th-century furnishings and

collectibles. *Pierre Passebon*, galerie du Passage, 22-26 Galérie Véro-Dodat, 75001 Paris; Tel: 01-42-36-01-13; galeriedupassage.com

APRIL 12–18: With a warm, contemporary ambiance conjured by designer Philippe Starck, the restaurant Brach, within the hotel Brach, is a stylish addition to the *comme il faut* 16th arrondissement. The inventive menu has a Mediterranean edge. Brach, 1-7 rue Jean Richepin, 75116 Paris; Tel: 01-44-30-10-00; brachparis.com

APRIL 19–25: In addition to the Luxembourg Gardens chair, Fermob offers a large collection of snazzy, colorful French patio and garden furniture available at stores worldwide. fermob.com

APRIL 26–MAY 2: One of the latest luxury hotels to debut in Paris, the Cour des Vosges overlooks the Place des Vosges, the oldest square in Paris. The hotel, part of the EVOK Hôtel Collection, offers 12 stately rooms and suites. *Cour des Vosges*, 19 place des Vosges, 75004 Paris; Tel: 01-42-50-30-30; courdesvosges.com

MAY 3–9: The extraordinary Jardins d'Étretat on Normandy's northern coast between Le Havre and Dieppe are a living horticultural work of art, created by the Russian-born landscape architect Alexandre Grivko. Seven themed gardens bloom with 150,000 different plants. *Les Jardins d'Étretat*, avenue Damilaville, 76790 Étretat; Tel: 02-35-27-05-76; etretatgarden.fr

MAY 17–23: Les Cigognes is a bucolic lodging offering simple but comfortable

SOURCES

rooms and wonderful home-cooked breakfasts. *Les Cigognes*, 211 bis chemin du Roy, 27680 Le Marais-Vernier; Tel: 06-68-03-39-39; lescigognesdumarais.fr

MAY 31–JUNE 6: Sarah Lavoine is a trendsetting Parisian interior designer with lines of stylish tableware and home furnishings. *Maison Sarah Lavoine*, 16 rue Gaillon, 75002 Paris; Tel: 01-42-60-60-40; maisonsarahlavoine.com

JUNE 7–13: The Domaine Saint-Clair Le Donjon Hotel is a charming, vine-covered hostelry surrounded by gardens overlooking the sea in Étretat. *Domaine Saint-Clair Le Donjon*, chemin de Saint-Clair, 76790 Étretat; Tel: 02-35-27-08-23; hoteletretat.com

JULY 19–25: A highlight along the north-west coast of the Cotentin Peninsula is the 17th-century Château de Vauville, with botanical gardens that thrive in the region's gentle microclimate. Open to the public from April through October. *Château de Vauville Botanical Garden*, 14 route des Fontaines, 50440 Vauville, La Hague; Tel 02-33-10-00-00; jardin-vauville.fr

AUGUST 9–15: A rooftop terrace offering not only views across Paris, but a kitchen garden and a barbecue chef for late-night munchies crowns the Brach hotel in the 16th arrondissement, designed by Philippe Starck and part of the EVOK Hôtel Collection. *Brach*, 1-7 rue Jean Richepin, 75116 Paris; Tel: 01-44-30-10-00; brachparis.com

AUGUST 23–29: Le Manoir offers an idyllic setting for a romantic Provençal retreat. *Le Manoir*, L'Oustau de Baumanière, Mas de Baumanière, 13520 Les Baux-de-Provence; Tel: 04-90-54-33-07; baumaniere.com

SEPTEMBER 6–12: Countess Priscilla and Count Antoine de Lamaze undertook a 10-year restoration of the 18th-century château and gardens à la française, returning Bois-Héroult to its original glory. The distinguished property is open to visitors June through September. *Le Domaine de Bois-Héroult*, 400 rue du Château, 76750 Bois-Héroult; Tel: 02-35-34-42-19; domaine-de-boisheroult.fr

SEPTEMBER 13–19: Château Figéac, a *Saint-Émilion Premier Grand Cru Classé* wine, is one of the most famous in Bordeaux. *Château Figéac*, 33330 Saint-Émilion; Tel: 05-57-24-72-26; chateau-figeac.com

SEPTEMBER 27–OCTOBER 3: Pierre Sauvage, an author and an expert on western rugs, is the owner of Casa Lopez, the sophisticated Paris interior design store, specializing in bold contemporary rugs and chic home design accessories. *Casa Lopez*, 27 boulevard Raspail, 75007 Paris; Tel: 01-42-22-66-04; casalopez.com

OCTOBER 11–15: Daniel Rozensztroch, designer and collector, is the artistic director of the trendsetting Paris design store Merci, and author, most recently, of *Spoon*, from Pointed Leaf Press. *Merci*, 111 boulevard Beaumarchais, 75003 Paris; Tel: 01-42-77-00-33; merci-merci.com

OCTOBER 25–31: The décor chez Mathias Toulemonde is by Paris interior designer Elodie Sire. *Elodie Sire*, 18 rue André Del Sarte, 75018 Paris; Tel: 01-42-02-82-72; dmesure.fr

NOVEMBER 8–14: Pierre-Jean Chalençon is one of the world's top experts on Empire style. *Pierre-Jean Chalençon, Cabinet d'Expertise Chalençon Empire*. chalencon2021@gmail.com

NOVEMBER 15–21: Jacqueline Socquet-Clerc Lafont's collection of demi-figurines, or half-dolls, in either porcelain or bisque portrays a variety of female figures from lavishly coiffed duchesses to demure flower girls. avocat@socquet-clerc.fr

NOVEMBER 29–DECEMBER 5: Rémy Le Fur is an art expert and founder of the renowned Paris auction house AuctionArt, Rémy Le Fur & Associés. *AuctionArt, Rèmy Le Fur & Associés*, 9 rue de Duras, 75008 Paris; Tel: 01-40-06-06-08; auctionartparis.com

DECEMBER 6–12: A chocolate-lover's dream, the Chocolaterie Bataille also offers fabulous hot chocolate as well as a variety of pastries. *Chocolaterie Bataille*, 14 boulevard Bansard des Bois, 61130 Bellême; Tel: 02-33-73-41-02; chocolateriebataille.wixsite.com/chocolateriebataille

DECEMBER 13–19: Les Fermes de Marie is a five-star, chalet-style resort with a fine restaurant and a soothing spa. *Les Fermes de Marie*, 163 chemin de la Riante Colline, 74120 Megève; Tel: 04-50-93-03-10; fermesdemarie.com

DECEMBER 20–26: Designer and French hairstylist to the stars Alexandre Zouari creates a line of glamorous hair accessories and jewelry popular with brides and fashionistas from Paris to Tokyo. alexandre-zouari-accessories.com